"Quick, effective marketing & motivational
training sessions driving you to success"

From Writing Poetry

To Crashing 747s

Vol. 22 In The *Sub 4 Minute Extra Mile* Series

by

Dr. Ted Ciuba

From Writing Poetry To Crashing 747s

Vol. 22 In The *Sub 4 Minute Extra Mile* Series

ISBN: 978-1478248279

by **Ted Ciuba**

www.ThinkRich.com
info@holomagic.com
Parthenon Marketing Inc
2400 Crestmoor Rd #36
Nashville TN 37215   USA

Orders & Enrollments
+1-877- *4 RICHES*
***
phone +1-615-662-3169
fax: +1-615-369-9749

 Contact Ted Ciuba about speaking for or training your group or organization.

Ted Ciuba is also the author of the incredible modernization and empowerment of Napoleon Hill's success classic, *Think & Grow Rich!*

Ted Ciuba
The New Think & Grow Rich
Author of Sub 4 Minute Extra Mile Series
Author of *The New Think And Grow Rich*

Tamara Doris

T.J. Rohleder

"This is **more than just a revamp with modern examples** - it radically transforms the vision by adding new gender, cross-cultural and international issues to the mix, including new material to include both science and genetics, as in the Quantum reality of accelerating income and wealth.

An excellent re-do of a classic financial inspirational guide."

"The writing is so much more applicable and understandable that I am literally forcing my friends, colleagues, and mastermind members to get their copies now!

Every page fills me with passion and revs me up!"

"I picked up Ted's book -- AND I WAS SHOCKED AND AMAZED! I sat there and began going through it ... and all of a sudden looked up and over 3 hours had gone by!!! I quickly read it from cover to cover within 2 days and then turned around and did it again! Ted has done a truly amazing thing, by totally re-writing this powerful classic. Every entrepreneur and business owner simply MUST have Ted's book!"

TABLE OF CONTENTS

CONTENTS

Vol. 22 In *The Sub 4 Minute Extra Mile* Series

FROM WRITING POETRY

TO CRASHING 747S

by

Dr. Ted Ciuba

Introduction: It Takes So Little To Excel

As an achiever, would you agree with me that you must go the extra mile? *I thought so...*

Surely you know if you do what average people do, you'll get the same kind of average results they do. And something tells me you're a cut above that!

And it's actually quite easy to stand out, because most people wouldn't dream of going the extra mile. But for you and me, while, yes, it takes something extra, yes, it takes drive and discipline.... The amazing thing is, it takes so *little* to excel!

Roger Bannister
Runs Sub 4 Minute Mile

After all, it's called the extra *mile*, not the extra *100 miles!*

Be that as it may, we're talking about the positive rewards that come to you in any economy by going the extra mile.

It was Roger Bannister who defied and redefined history by running the sub 4 minute mile.

And the amazing thing is that Bannister did NOT spend the countless hours and hours practicing that conventional training would guide him to. He gave it what he could... In his busy pre-med Oxford schedule he took a mere 30 minutes out of his daily lunch hour to train and run. And with that he set a world record that had towered 3,000 years!

He ushered in a new era of possibility. Though no one had *ever* broken it, within 2 1/2 years time of Bannister's record-breaking, seemingly unachievable sub 4 minute mile, 18 others were doing it.

And how did he do it?... It wasn't a function of *time*. Conventional sports training encompasses hours on an almost daily basis, not 30 minutes!!

It was *intention*. Roger Bannister, in the short, focused, regular, intense, intended few minutes per day he wrested from his busy Oxford pre-med studies was throwing himself into the sport. He gave it everything he could, as an additional interest and pursuit in his life...

You see, when Roger Bannister suffered the ignominious defeat of coming in 5th place in the 1952 Olympics, right then and there, he determined to be the first human to run the sub 4 minute mile!

It was just a "thought". It's just another instance and undisputable illustration, my friend, of the power of intention powered by determination.

Moments before 6 pm on 6 May 1954, he takes a breath of vision and determination. He feels it! He confides to his pacemakers "The sub 4 minute attempt is on!"

Short moments later the shot is fired... The runners are off!! Roger Bannister breaks the string at the end of the mile in 3 minutes, 59 seconds, and 4/10's, trailblazing into the sub 4 minute mile age!

Recognition Point!! - This was NOT an unintended event! Recognition point!! Little efforts, little accomplishments - short, focused, regular, intense, intended training sessions - gear into colossal events!

Also note how little it takes to stand waaay beyond the competition! Roger Bannister redefined history in one evening... And he did it only with the razor's edge of difference, 1/10 of a second over 1/2 of a second!!!

This didn't happen by circumstance... Roger Bannister didn't "drift" over the finish line into the annals of history... It was the thing he geared all his intentions to accomplish, even though he didn't spend hours and hours a day in the quest to achieve it.

Which gives rise to the name of this series, The *Sub 4 Minute Extra Mile* Series...

Now you, honoring Roger Bannister's history-setting accomplishments and methods, can make the same kind of history-breaking progress in sub 4 minutes a day! Defy the status quo in short, focused, regular, intense, intended training sessions and redefine what's possible and what you accomplish!

OUTTHINK YOUR WEALTH

In the multi-faceted, eclectic, holomagic philosophy I teach my friends, family members, clients, affiliates, associates, and protégés, marketing is always a big part of it.

I saw a headline just the other day, and I'm a sucker for a good headline. I recommend that you develop that same sense, because we're all in the selling business, and we all can optimize.

That is, here's the theory: if you're running an ad and that ad costs you $1,000 a month in a certain publication, that ad costs you $1,000 a month whether it brings you one customer or 1,000 customers. The headline has been proven to be the most effective single element of what gets a person to read an ad.

So again, optimization: if you get a better headline on an ad and you're paying the same no matter what, you get more out of it. You get more responses to your ad. You sell more product. You make more profit. ☺ So become headline sensitive, and aware.

You'll get to where you love them - everywhere you go. So this headline says, "Outthink Your Health!" Now, that's outthink your *physical* health. They're coming at it clearly from the mindset, from the mind-body connection.

Whereas optimism, positive expectancy, engagement in your definite chief aim—all these things make for a life that's more engaging, that's more balanced, where we have better habits, where we live longer, with lower cholesterol and lower blood pressure. Everybody knows this today, they just chose to come from a different direction.

You know, "out think". It's kind of a military metaphor, a "we're going to outsmart them" kind of thing. That's an approach that's out there in marketing all the time. It stays popular. So outthink your health... And the way to do that is to be young, positive inside.

And it hit me that just one letter, a lot of times, can change a headline. How about "Outthink Your Wealth"? Your *wealth*, as in your money? It's the same identical process.

The title of Napoleon Hill's famous book is *Think and Grow Rich*. That's obviously outthinking. That's really thinking deep, beyond, thinking til you understand, thinking where you go to mentors to get clarification and guidance, thinking aloud in Mastermind groups that help you, thinking where you're contributing.

It's also thinking where you're doing more than an average person does, thinking where you're in action, thinking where you are persistent no matter what, even if you have to adjust.

The mind-*environment* connection. What you see is what you've created to this point. Now, you can create something entirely new, much more spectacular from this point forward, and the only place you can go forward from is the point you're at right now.

Be that as it may, outthink your wealth. It's the same process.

Grab hold of your thinking processes. Install the proper characteristics, trades, attitudes, skills, abilities, sensitivities that are warp and woof of this philosophy and you will outthink your wealth. You will create good wealth as easily as you create good health.

THERE IS A RHYTHM WHEREVER YOU ARE, ADJUST

Myself, I love them both for what they are, but there *are* two dramatic differences in geography that not everyone knows about—because most people have not traveled, and certainly have not traveled broadly. The difference occurs between the equatorial regions versus the northern and the southern regions.

In the northern and the southern regions, we experience seasons, the four seasons. In the equatorial regions, these things just do not exist, because there's not enough tilt of the Earth's axis...and it's not really the actual tilt of the axis, it's the tilt of the axis in relation to its rotation around the Sun. You're certainly educated enough to understand that.

But it affects life. For instance, I myself have a place in both Nashville, Tennessee, which is in the southeastern part of the United States, and I have a place in La Ciudad de Panamá—in Panamá City, Panamá. In Panamá, they define things in two seasons, the dry and the wet season.

And this is not unique, by the way, to Panamá. There are a lot of equatorial-oriented countries that define life that way. Because remember, we're talking about equatorial versus the north and the south—it's above or below the tropics line.

The tropics live a life where seasons don't change. It rains or it doesn't. The others above and below the tropical lines live a life of four seasons.

Now, what's the big, important take-home point of all this exploration, clarification and understanding about this particular point? The point is it is what it is. In other words, whichever environment you're in, the physical environment is going to be what the physical environment is.

We talk about *think* and grow/create what you want. Well, we're certainly not talking about changing the environment. Let's not be crazy about it.

What we *are* talking about is the fact that, wherever you are, you must accept what is. It's the conditions of the place, it's the local color, it's the food. Do they have more barbecue or do they have more tacos, or more pasta—you catch my drift? The human things, the important things, the value of what you create, is always up to you.

But as you move through this world, the world does seem to divide climatically into those worlds who have four seasons and those worlds who have wet and dry. In other words, there's a *rhythm* wherever you are. Adjust, adapt, celebrate—and let's go make money.

PROFIT FROM THE "AND MUST HAVE" ITEMS

Whatever you sell, think of the "and must have" items. For instance, it's not ironic and it *is* ironic that I recently went to Wal-Mart to buy myself a simple bicycle in one of the cities I frequent, just so I could get around campus, so to speak. But, I can't buy *just* a bicycle—you know that won't work.

Myself, I must have gloves. This is just one of my personal items. I do a lot of keyboarding, so I protect the health of my fingers. I always have gloves. Now, not everybody would need gloves, but every idiot would need a helmet. Even idiocy could get worse, you know...

So, when I buy that bicycle someone's got to sell me a helmet, and someone's got to sell me gloves. *Someone!* Should it be the person who sells me the bicycle or not? And further on, holy smoko, I'm thinking about riding the bicycle to a restaurant—I'd better have a lock so I can lock this thing up.

Now, who should sell me that lock—the person who sells me the bicycle? Or should they *inconvenience* me, and make me drag myself to some other place and try and find it and buy it there?

Now, this is a metaphor for your business. When you are selling one thing, what are the other "and must have" items people need to fully utilize the product or service you're selling? Now, you know Wal-Mart doesn't manufacture all their items. In other words, if you're selling a product or service and it needs another related product or service to fully solve the customer's problem or agenda, it doesn't have to be *your* product or service!

It can be someone else's service with your referral or affiliate link. You deserve to make money when you bring business to the table, and every business out there will gladly pay you for that increased revenue. That's the whole thing about it.

So it's a real simple process. Think through what I've said whenever you're thinking of offering a new product or service.

Provide the service today's savvy and time-pressed consumers want – they want a solution to their entire problem, not a part of it. Make strategic alliances with vendors of the "and must have" items your product or service needs for optimal performance, and make more money!

NOTES

Item / passage / page	Insight	Action

FOR NOW HE'S IN LASALLE DETENTION CENTER

I once knew a guy, met him, talked with him, at a show—we were at work on a weekend. This was just two days before he killed himself in a high-speed auto accident. Only a few of us knew what really happened, because what got reported in the media was *not* what really happened.

Be that as it may, I knew him. I knew what was going on. And there was a sadness there. And I've known a number of people like that. I know another guy who played Russian roulette *by himself*—I mean, there was nothing he could possibly gain, as with another person. You know, like there's two of us and we each bequeath our fortunes to the other if I'm the one who goes.

Suicide.

I got another friend who did it—and by the way, I'm not abnormal. I'm normal enough. Men like high-speed auto accidents.

And I have a friend who, just a couple weeks ago as I write this, was picked up by INS, the Immigration Service, and as I understand it he's right now waiting in LaSalle Detention Center in New Orleans for deportation to Honduras.

Well, I'm going to tell you, that there were a *lot* of things crazy about *that* night. I did happen to see him, and I did happen to see his companion who was with him when he got stopped. It was 1:30 in the morning. Hey, can I tell you that he was asking for it?

I didn't say 1:30 in the afternoon, I didn't say 9:00 at night. I said it was 1:30 in the morning when he got stopped. What was he doing driving, blitzed out of his mind? And that brings up a whole 'nother thing about social responsibility and all, but what I'm saying is that I saw the guy...and I knew he was on a collision course for disaster. By the way, that's the same thing I knew about the friend who did a high-speed auto wreck.

Success, as Anthony Robbins says, leaves clues. So does failure. The seeds of disaster come *before* the disaster.

So think, brother, sister, friend. If you ever find yourself getting into such a position, reach out, reach out, because you've got Mastermind partners, you've got people who love you and care for you, public and private. You don't have to suffer it alone.

Don't be resistant. I saw it coming the night my friend got picked up. I begged him, pleaded with him, "Please do not drive!" I saw him at midnight. He came, he bothered me, molested me, and he went driving. I gave him a place to stay, *everything* I could, but he brought it on himself. Now, he knows that. He will survive. It's a lesson for you and me.

There are many who will not survive, when we see the early signs of whatever it is that we're not going to like. That's the time when we can still take control and gather hold of the situation.

Because for now, my friend is in LaSalle Detention Center—and there isn't anything he has to say about his own destiny.

BE VIGILANT - ROW, ROW, ROW YOUR BOAT!

I know this guy...I saw it coming. I've written before about my buddy from Honduras who got picked up by INS and shipped back home. After nine years here, by the way, he had a life. But you know, I saw it coming, because of the dissatisfaction in his life.

Remember how we talk about *think* and grow rich? We say—although it's not our main focus of emphasis in teaching—think and grow *poor* also. Or think poorly, get involved in problems. In other words, the way you're thinking will, and does, manifest in your environment.

Which is why we who are conscious live with vigilance. We really do have to stay on top of things. If things are going in a way that is not conducive to our health and wellbeing—if we're arguing more with our spouse, we're not seeing our children, we're getting overweight, we're having sexual freedom, we're into drugs or alcoholism—we have to stop it while we can.

I've counseled with and coached with thousands and thousands and thousands of people. And I will say that there are, and have been, a few who didn't see it coming. But the reality is that the majority saw it coming. This boy did too.

In fact, one of his family members said (and it was in family conversation, I don't want you to take it the wrong way), "It's good that he got picked up and he's getting shipped back to Honduras, because none of us had the money to send his cadaver back."

In other words, they all recognized he was on a path of self destruction. It's not just for rock stars, by the way. And it does come from an unhappiness.

And you know, in this man's regard, I happen to know the guy—I happen to have been close to him, and I happen to have been in his shoes in another way... And no, it's no miracle, we're all human. Not everybody's *been* in these shoes, but he was hurting for a love. He's a young man, 28 years old, who left his country nine years ago. It's just not that easy in this country for an uneducated, subsistence-earning illegal immigrant.

But Nature... It's the time, it's the flocking syndrome, it's the nesting thing. He was hurting.

And the day he got picked up, he displayed such egregious behavior they couldn't help but pick him up. That's the true story of what happened. You see, *think and grow poor* works if you don't work the think and grow rich concept. He wasn't aware of what was going on inside him – driven by it though he was...

What happened was nothing more than the end result of poor actions he was taking because he was thinking and feeling so poorly himself inside... The climax – everything led to this dramatic turn of events. And if it hadn't of been this drama, it would have been another...

But not to get swept downstream with negative energy... Because when people are on the positive side of the stream, I see it coming also.

And *that's* what you must do: be vigilant - row, row, row your boat. Know where you're going, stay on target, and defeat, deflect, and mirror off any doubt, any lack of self confidence that could lead you otherwise.

DRINKING A CUP OF COFFEE ON A VERY DREARY LOOKING DAY

Eight a.m. Monday morning, Nashville, Tennessee. It's a rainy autumn day, what many people would call a dreary day. Driving with the headlights on...need the lights on inside. And many people have been jumping to it for the last couple of hours, getting ready, getting the kids off to school, getting on to the jobsite.

And there's a group I've been friends and associates with for about 10 years now. A photocopy company. Last week was not a good week for the employees of the photocopy company. I'm thinking about how they are today, waking up on their first workday without employment. People of all ages, people of all skills, specific and general.

You see, what happened was, a competitive photocopy company came in and made the owner—who's been running the place for the last 32 years with mostly the same crew—an offer. The man hasn't made any money in over two years; I know that because, again, I'm close to it, I'm doing some consulting. And so it was a good time for him to get out.

Well, the competitors who bought him out have a meeting on Monday last. They tell the employees, "All is well, don't worry, we have to pass around the personnel file, and here's some applications you've got to fill out. But, everything's fine. We're going to send our crew in, and begin an integration process, and we want you to really show them everything you can."

Well, come Friday right before lunch, they call them all and say, "Look, you need to get down here to the office at 3 p.m. Even if you're on vacation, you need to be here." A young MBA type opened the meeting saying, "We apologize, this is the hardest part of our job, but as of 5 p.m. you no longer have a job here."

"There's an envelope on your desk, and we've got boxes and extra crew, and we'll help you clean out your desk, and you can go home. Be out of here before 5pm. Your career here is over."

That envelope had a check that amounted to two weeks "severance pay"... And they didn't tell them explicitly, but scuttlebutt ran the vine, and everybody knew it meant, "If you take that envelope, and if you sign that letter drafted by our attorney, you get a check. If you don't—it'll go the other way."

And then they began herding them out, helping the ex-employees (carelessly) pack boxes. Helping them carry the boxes to their cars... Some of these people had worked there for 14, 15, 16 years. It had been a very stable place, and they found out at 3:00 they had no job come 5 pm. No work to report to on Monday.

I can't help but think about them, because I know where they'll be. They're normally in that busy hustle, but today they're looking out, at 8 a.m., out of their own home-based situation, drinking a cup of coffee on a very *dreary*-looking day that could just perfectly match the mood they may have.

YOU COULD HAVE DONE A LOT WORSE, BUT YOU COULDN'T HAVE DONE MUCH BETTER

There's no shortage of remarkable people—and there's no shortage of remarkable people that I know, live, move, and have my existence with. I *enjoy* the world of achievers. Anybody could tune into the news and find remarkable people.

But I've got a friend who started off as a client, someone who bought one of my books. He came to me because we were actually close in physical proximity, and we started up a relationship. And he's been talking about his son-in-law, who is connected in the real estate industry. A young guy.

And the other day I got to meet him. We all had lunch together, we had a business meeting—I'm helping them create some products. And I met this young, ambitious, good-looking, trim man who is on the move, who is creating things. Well, this other gentleman and I are now of the, ahem, *grandfather* age, and it does change your outlook somewhat.

Later on, we got together and I told him, "You know, your son-in-law really is impressive." He was; fact, no issue. Here's what I said that really lighted his heart, and it was *true*. And hope that the Gods can make it true in most instances in your life, as they have in mine.

I told him, "You know, you're a fortunate man to have that man as your son-in-law." The man who's caring for his daughter, you understand. Again, we've got these certain things that are important to us!

I said, "You could've done a lot worse, but you couldn't have done much better."

May they say the same thing about you.

NOTES

Item / passage / page	Insight	Action	

SLUGGING AROUND 100 POUND BAGS OF CONCRETE IN YOUR SIXTIES

One of my most ambitious, actually on-target clients (because you'd be surprised, not everybody who pays follows through) is a man who's over sixty. His exact age I don't know, but he's working to get out of his concrete profession.

Concrete, ai! Now, thank God he's in good health. But this guy is carrying around, slugging around, 100-pound bags of concrete in his sixties! Yeah, you better *believe* he's an ambitious guy. You better *believe* he's paying attention.

You might want to think about your *own* future. You see, a lot of the people are working because they love the work. Well, that's okay in your 20s or 30s, but...

Well, let me put it this way... There's an industry we call *education*—and we always said to ourselves that, in that industry, well, we can work into our 60s and 70s because we're not slugging around 100-pound bags of concrete.

But can you imagine?!

I helped my daughter move just a few months ago, and it was a small move, yet it was wearisome on me. I don't think you want to be slugging around 100-pound bags of concrete when you're in your 60s, even if you *are* physically fit. The Gods just haven't made the human body to continue to do that at that level, at that time.

Think about it. What business can you become an owner of, an entrepreneur of, that you can put into motion, that could care for you at that time—rather than you doing the work of working?

NOTES

Item / passage / page	Insight	Action

IT'S HOW WE LIVE AND HOW WE LOVE IN THE PRESENT

You've heard the statement "a marriage made in heaven." Well, as I write this, my dear friend lost her husband just yesterday. And believe me—all of her dreams, all of her goals, all of her ambitions, all of her activities, have been centered around and connected with this man who no longer is here. In an instant. With no warning or symptoms.

The man was discovered nude in his living quarters, seated in the lotus position, bowed over, apparently having departed in his morning meditations.

You bet it's going to be a game changer. And it just amazes me how rapidly, how dramatically, a game changer curve-ball pitch can come at us as human beings.

And this is not the first time. She lost a daughter who was 23 years of age, who just was sick. The pharmacy screwed up - more specifically, some particular pharmacist - and gave her medicine that was way more powerful than what she was supposed to have been taking. That's where they "found the blame" on that one. She's not a blame kind of person.

Game changer. Now, of course she needs a few days to grieve... Let's give her grace. But she's forced to change everything in her life radically... Again.

Well, I feel for her because of the suddenness of it. On the other hand, she's still young enough where she can bounce back—and she will. Who knows? Two or three years from now, she could even have another spouse. This was not her first spouse, but I do know the stories of their fairytale romance.

And I know the chivalric nature he always treated her in. And I know it's not easy to find a replacement for that guy. That's true. While I can feel pain for her, and I'm grieving for her - and him, too, but, of course, I'm thinking more of the one who's still living—I do know she will get on with it, because there is no other option in the final analysis.

We celebrate, we live to the max, the good times we have. And, like I said, everything in her life was connected to, with, and around this noble man.

Hey, there is no security in life. Having her life connected with him is the way it *should* be. That is the way of living life to the max: not of being fearful of what *may* happen in the future, even though we all know it may. And we know we'll adjust.

It's how we live and how we love in the present. It's always changing even as we move forward. And they call it a present for a very good reason.

OPPORTUNITY IS ALWAYS PRESENT

The great impresario, the great businessmen of the department store industry, J.C. Penney, is quoted to have said,

> "Give me a stock clerk with a goal,
> and I'll give you a person who will make history.
> Give me a person without a goal,
> and I'll give you a stock clerk."

Absolutely! J.C. Penney was the walking embodiment of this, as was Ray Kroc, who built an industry in hamburgers, of all things. Turned into McDonald's. As was Col. Harland Sanders, our friend from Kentucky, who at an advanced age in his 60s began a new business that turned into Kentucky Fried Chicken. And it goes on and on.

Andrew Carnegie came here as young man, an immigrant to this country, and became the richest man in America for the years he was here—and gave away countless millions of dollars. He still does to this day.

No, no, it's not in the opportunity. Edwin Barnes showed up at Thomas Edison's plant and got a job, as Edison had mentioned because of the attitude that he clearly saw in the young man's face. He didn't get any encouragement, though, until he put his foot forward, he put his hand forward, he stepped forward with confidence at the right time, when he saw the opportunity, and said, "Mr. Edison, I can solve that problem for you."

You see, it's not in opportunity. Oh, by the way; Edison had a sales force who was supposed to sell that machine he had invented. They couldn't be bothered... They thought it was a dumb idea. Acting on that one impulse of thought made Edwin Barnes rich.

"It's in the man, not the land," not to be sexist—that's just an old sales saying. How much fire in your belly do you have? How bad do you want it? Because opportunity is always available. It's will you reach up, identify it, grasp hold, set history, make income? Will *you* do it? Now you tell me, and tell yourself—I want you to talk to yourself here. Are you ready to do it *now*?

NOTES

Item / passage / page	Insight	Action

I WANT TO MAKE IT BURN AS BRIGHTLY AS POSSIBLE

I'm sure, as an achiever, you'll appreciate this quote from George Bernard Shaw as deeply as I do.

"This is the true joy in life: the being used for a purpose recognized by yourself as a mighty one.

TThe being a force of nature instead of a feverish, selfish clod of ailments and grievances, complaining that the world will not devote itself to making you happy.

"I am of the opinion that my life belongs to the whole community, and as long as I live it is my privilege to do for it whatever I can. I want to be thoroughly used up when I die, for the harder I work, the more I live.

"I rejoice in life for its own sake. Life is no brief candle to me; it is a sort of a splendid torch, which I have hold of for the moment. And I want to make it burn as brightly as possible before handing it over to future generations."

Wow. If only we would think like that, if only we would take this into our morning meditations, if only we would get it into our character, as George Bernard Shaw did, as many artists, business people, mothers, teachers, evangelists, botanists have, as many people have done.

The *exceptional* ones have realized they are not living their own lives, but live the life of HoloCosm, the life of HoloMagic. They are a representative of the Force, with the opportunity and the *gracious*, the *glad* passion to contribute something to that force. To make the torch burn as brightly as they can in the few moments it is their turn to carry it, and to hand it off to the next runner in the human continuity when they've run their distance.

NOTES

Item / passage / page	Insight	Action	

FROM WRITING POETRY TO CRASHING 747'S

I remember exactly where I was at the change of the millennium. It was 31 December 31 1999 combined with and reaching over to 1 January 2000. I've often wondered how many careers were destroyed—or should've been.

If you remember back then we were involved in the Y2K mania/pandemonium. We were frightened ablazes to death that security systems weren't going to work, that airplanes would lose their navigation systems mid-flight, and that Star Wars was going to *KABOOM!* And that *even* our personal laptops wouldn't work.

Now, I know we didn't all have laptops back then as we do today, but you catch my drift. I remember where I was: I was about 100 miles east of Bogotá, Colombia, in the Andes Mountains, on the side of a mountain. Like all good Latinos, we, of course, celebrated well and brought in the New Year.

There were a lot of different Colombian customs I was new to, and I loved every minute of it. And in the morning, I woke about 7 am when my eyes popped open. I go to the front porch where the mountain Eastern sun is shining in full glory. There's a chair I sit myself down in and - I'm in flow! Very cool location, after all, on a pretty cool day... And I'm writing a little poetry to my significant other - who I'm there with!...

And *my* laptop's working perfectly fine. Hmmm...

There was no radio that we had at that remote distance, and at that time they didn't have the same worldwide connectivity we do today with cell phones. Of course, now I've got a cell phone worldwide and a laptop connection worldwide that works most places, but it doesn't always work when you get remote.

We didn't know if the rest of the world existed or not. Of course I had my suspicions it did, though I wasn't to find out for *sure* until we got back on the road and in touch with radio signals.

Wow, okay, so we go from writing poetry to crashing 747's all in the same change of the year, all in the same threat.

 Interesting how we humans can *exaggerate* what we focus on and we can manipulate, and "hypulate" something we want to sell. And we must, as consumers, guard against being over-hypulated. I never bought into the Y2K—I never did. I read the explanations, I bought a software patch, and it was installed in less than three seconds.

That was the extent of the Y2K, and some people crested it to an information marketing fortune. Of course it crashed on them, immediately after the new millennium came.

You know what? It was the same exaggerated mania they had last millennium. Imagine that!

THE WORLD IS A REACTION TO YOU

In the audio version of this, you'd hear a bunch of dogs barking right about now (and me woofing back at them). I'll tell you what, man, that's a *bad* group of dogs there. I'm in my own neighborhood walking by, and every time I go by they're always very, should we say, aggressive? They bark and they cause trouble.

I never noticed it until just now, which is why I'm just taking the time to write this article—but when I go by, my character changes from peaceful to guarded, and from not even thinking about anything else in the world to getting back at them – "Whoof, whoof!"

And you know, it's just the way it is. Here I am, walking in the neighborhood, and dogs come, and I react. It's a lesson of life—it's not just a neighborhood event. I mean, it's not a big deal to bark back at dogs that are within a fence, right? But they are aggressive, and I *am* reacting.

I'm walking down the street with Cloud Number 9 stamped on my forehead, getting my exercise with my Nike tennis shoes on—which is a success story all of itself that I do know that you know about and want to know about - and suddenly, I'm in counter-aggression reacting to *them*.

Well, it's not a big deal that I'm reacting to dogs – and that's not the point of this lesson. The lesson is however *we* as individuals—that means you, that means me, it means everybody as an individual—present ourselves, we are going to elicit a reaction from people who otherwise would not even be concerned about our existence, our program, our platform. However we present ourselves to the world.

Whatever our vibration is, whether it is one of anger or one of peace, we're going to elicit a reaction.

So, do you understand *where* you're coming from?

See, you do have choices, and it takes a lot of work to think it through. It takes reflection. But you get to decide who you'd like to be—what kind of impression you'd make. And it's like Henry Ford says, "Think you can, think you can't, either way, you're right."

It's like the story goes, in which someone asks, "Well, what were the people like where you came from?" And then when the person answers you either they were horrible or they were splendid—then they reveal, "They're just like that here." Because the world is a reaction to you, the giver.

GOOD MARKETING IN THE INVESTIGATIVE FIELD

I'm not saying we don't need the investigative sciences, but I don't mind admitting to you that, for the most part, I'm much more proactive, creative, moving forward, being excited. I'm not living in the past. I'm not trying to dig up muck on people, and I don't have a consuming interest in what they did when, where, and why.

But, I tell you what—there *is* one company in the investigative field that I patronize. It's called Thomas Publications. If you go to the web it's PImall.com - that PI stands for "private investigator." And the only reason I do that is because of the small hand-held recorder I use to record my articles, to record certain notes. They're the only source of the high quality, compact technically advanced audio equipment I need. You can't get what I need at the discount electronics super stores.

Not as a snoop device, mind you, but I do need quality, reliable, compact, portable recording equipment.

It's very convenient; it fits in a pocket.

Now, their usual audience is investigators, and the intent of this piece is that it would be surreptitious. Policemen use this, and of course, the mark doesn't even know they're being recorded. And other investigators use it, too. It can be hidden, it's got a good pick-up, and it comes across with good quality.

These things are routinely used the same way in high stakes business negotiations. Ever hear of *corporate espionage?* Well, again, that's not the way I use it, although I *have* used it to record very significant conversations I wanted to save.

To me, it's used in marketing. Many things I do, I don't get a 2nd shot at... I'm not capturing notes, I'm laying tracks, so I must have a voice recorder that makes high quality captures I can use in products and presentations. Then, because I'm so often on the go, it must be very portable. This thing fits in my pants pocket – no bulge at all.

So I ordered another one, because nothing lasts forever. I got it and they sent me these brochures and catalogues. Advertising the kind of stuff that serves their industry. Billy clubs, brass knuckles, extra gun holsters, stun guns, you know—all this stuff you need if you're in that field, I reckon.

I scan it and trash it. And then this one flyer, a little bifold flyer, comes up and I recognize something that is in my industry, a headline...

Investigate Why You Should Join NAIS!

I didn't have any idea what NAIS was, but I said, "Whoa! Look, that's a good headline," because they're using industry specific terms — investigate - in marketing to their industry.

They sent it to me like I was a typical customer of theirs. And then I looked a little closer because the marketing had caught my eye, and I said, "Oh—NAIS is National Association of Investigative Specialists."

Now isn't that a double whammy of a headline for their target market? And a play on words? Something that might appeal to and delight their target market?

So I have to give them credit, they're doing some good marketing. Enjoy and learn from everywhere you go!

YOU'VE GOT TO LIVE FOR TODAY AND YOU'VE GOT TO PREPARE FOR TOMORROW

We are a custodian of our gifts. The responsibility we have is to be a good steward.

You see, life is loaned to us and it's a demand note, and we don't know when the person that gave it, it would presumably be God, when God is going to demand that the debt be paid. When God's going to demand an accounting. And it may seem capricious knowing this, you know we could die tomorrow and it could say well why should I plan for the life of living with my kids, grandkids and great-grand children at the same time?

The ironies of life. You've got to live for today and you've got to prepare for tomorrow at the same time because you don't know. That is the message. Life is loaned to you; there will be an accounting asked of you. And I'm not talking about you'll go to the mythical heaven or hell, that stuff is, in my point of view, doesn't even apply. But certainly, between you and HoloCosm, between you and the Cosmic, there will be an accounting. And there will be did you contribute, did you help others, did you make the world a better place? Or did you just merely survive? Or worse yet, were you on the take?

Think these things over. Become the person you want to be. Recognize how important it is to contribute and to express your gift *today*! Because, even if you live to 113, life is short. But you may not even live 13 more days, or 13 more minutes. You may not live 13 more seconds. What do you leave behind? What are they gonna write, what are they gonna say about *you?*

NOTES

Item / passage / page	Insight	Action

THERE HAVE BEEN BIG ADVANCES OVER BRAIN ENTRAINMENT

In nature, as in physics there's a phenomenon known as entrainment. It's like when a man brings in 400 grandfather clocks into a room, and it's chaotic because they're all doing their own thing, but you give it a few weeks and they all tick, tick, tick in rhythm. They have entered into entrainment with each other.

So, we do the same thing in personal development in the programs that are kind of meditative, trancelike, or hypnotic. We play a music that matches the optimal rhythm which, when the human mind (brainwaves) synchronizes or "entrains" with it, allows it to access higher abilities.

Now I have no issues with brainwave entrainment. It's often also commonly called brain entrainment. It's good. This thing's been around for a long time. The issues I have with it though, are, while it's not obsolete, its old technology.

There's a new system out called Neuro Synergist Sound Technology®. It's way advanced over merely brain entrainment. It includes several technologies, including entrainment and nlp.

Compare it with—hey, the principles of flight have never changed since we took off at Kittyhawk, right? But don't you think an F-16 fighter jet is a lot more sophisticated?

So this is what happens is brainwave entrainment hasn't gone bad, but there's so much more that can happen now. See brainwave entrainment is a rhythm. But there's sounds, there's frequencies that, with the passage of time we've been able to discover and develop to benefit humans. Now I'm not even going to go into what NLP could do in a program, and sub-audible messages, because those are also part of it, too. But I'm talking about the uniquenesses of the science of neurosynergist sound technology® right now.

Way more than entrainment, let me give you a few instances of what it is...

You can have affirmations spoken in one ear, spoken in another ear, different ones, first person, second person. Male voice speaking, female voice that connects with your yang energy. This is all part of the technology. You have a mother's heartbeat in the womb, when you put that on an audio program, video program, it can really break up, wake up, certain things. Sparkling waters mean something to the human animal.

The sound thrower, part of the technology, it'll throw sound around, around, around, around, around and around and it enchants; it's a novel thing that enchants you. The spring call of morning birds shown to foster spectacular points of change. And you're led up and down the brainwave frequency through beta, alpha, theta and delta -

whereas without neurosynergist sound technology® you normally only get from beta into alpha.

Here's a few more things that relate to specific sounds and frequencies you encounter in neurosynergist sound technology®:

A specific frequency of crickets that effects the brain stem and helps change your belief systems ...

The audible compression of the pulsing of the sun which acts to strengthen the powers of your corpus callosum...

The audible compression of various "sounds" from space induce connection with Universal Intelligence and your own higher consciousness...

A mother's heartbeat in the womb which awakens your deep primal brain to new information...

The songs of whales and dolphins engage your emotions and your higher consciousness...

The sounds of evening frogs stimulate the human immune system...

The chants of Tibetan Monks and bowl which open spaces for quantum shifts in your perception of reality...

I could go on and on, and on, there's more. You're just getting the idea we need to go beyond brainwave entrainment now, to go into the next generation of personal development change.

THAT I CONTINUE TO CONTRIBUTE TO HUMANITY

This is one of those articles, one of those statements where I'm not really sure what it's supposed to mean—but I am *sure* it means for you as well as for me.

I was looking through some old boxes the other day, cleaning out the attic. I've done a recent move, so I was sorting things into a new life. And I got to this box that I hadn't opened in years—and I found some poetry I had written.

Now today, as a gentrified man, I'm not writing much poetry. I'm really involved in marketing, hypnosis, empowerment, transformation - those kinds of topics. But back then, I was interested in—well, let me put it this way: I was more driven by the fairer sex than I am today.

Not that this poem I'm about to share has anything to do with the fairer sex...it doesn't. But that was the conceptualization, why I was writing more poetry then.

And I carry it with me to a family gathering, folded in my jacket pocket. The amazing thing is, I wrote this poem 28 years ago, my own hand inscribes 1982-05-19 —and it was my daughter who pointed it out to me.

I gift it now to you...

> I know my words and my wealth
> Will not accompany me through the door of death,
> But I've more than a selfish drive to produce and prosper.
> I write to benefit humanity.
>
> I build and contribute *now*, while I am *here,* alive and grinning,
> So that even when I wear a gray engraved stone
> My existence may continue to contribute to humanity,
> Much like the dead tree in the forest,
>
> Rotting now many years, once a tremendous oak
> Whose rusty remnants today support colonies of green lichen and moss,
> Many white and brown mushrooms, and armies of brown burrowing earthworms
> The whole of its reclining length -
> Contributing yet because it was healthy and successful
> And grew to great heights during its life.
>
> I only pray that in God's service, please continue

> To bless me with healthy rain,
> And that I do not refuse the drink of living life to its limits
> So that, like the dead oak in its forest,
> Dead, I continue to contribute to humanity.

"Ooh, 28 years ago," my daughter said, "that's interesting."

Indeed. But the mystery grows... Interesting?!! It might have been interesting if it was in the 28th year... But it was 28 years on the day we discovered the poem together! Where we kind of folk gather, we call that holomagic.

Yes, it is. You see, I chose a magical life over a calculated life. Not to say one's better than the other. Be true to yourself. Contribute to humanity.

CLEARLY THE MARKET SPEAKS

Nobody likes to spend money in an unfruitful venture. A marketer is actually in the business of designing and purchasing advertising to get the message out to a large number of qualified prospects so the leads can come in, so the sales team can get the money coming in, so they can pay the costs of sales, production and fulfillment, the operational, expenses, office expenses, administrative, taxes—and still turn a profit.

So let's talk about how important marketing is.

We have a saying in our office: "Clearly the market speaks." Now, the first time we ever uttered that, it was, "Clearly, the market has spoken," because we were watching tests. But now we do enough tests—for example, is it a digital product or is it a physical product, is it $97.00 or is it $67.00?

It instituted a was of life for our institution. Does it have three bonuses, or does it have seven? Or if it has three, what are those three? What is the headline? The blazing headline is the number one thing every marketer tests.

And so, of course, "clearly the market has spoken" is adequate for a single event, a single test. But it turns into "clearly the market speaks." It's a matter of what we call *optimization*. You don't know, in your greatest feelings of genius state, what the market actually will prefer.

I've seen one headline outpull another by 19 times. Now, that can be the difference between $100 or $1,900, or between $100,000 and $1.9 million.

Take your pick.

Yes, this may be an extreme case, but it's not a rare case. How much bang do you want to get for your advertising dollar? Do the math. Assume the advertising budget to make that second range of figures mentioned above was $30,000. That's what you, as the business person invest.

Let's consider the unoptimized version of your sales message as the one that makes your company $100,000. That might seem good when you pencil out a 333% gain on the project. But this is business, not investing... There's lots of other expenses and money needs in a business.

When, investing the same $30,000, but with a sales message that's been tested and tweaked, from headlines to storylines, and all points in between, and that best-of-the-best, optimized sales message goes out, you're not gambling at all... That $1.9 million income to investment ratio pencils out as a 6,333% gain.

Impressive difference, but forget the percentages, for a moment... Let's talk real world dollars. $1.9 million will pay a lot more expenses and give you a LOT more profits than $100,000 will, wouldn't you agree?

That's what's available to you as an entrepreneur that would never be available to you as an employee. The opportunity to "mind your business" and strategically leverage your way to riskless profits.

Do a small test... If you ask the impartial market, it will give you a definitive answer. Then, roll out, invest more following up on more leads with the variables that have proven to be most effective – proven themselves on the battle lines of today to make money. That's the wise use of leverage.

The issue is, test! You'll never know this, nor get these kind of dramatic results if you just shoot blind.

Test variables. You obviously start with the ones that affect things most—headline, price, positioning of the offer, color. Keywords, demographics, targeting...

By the way, even while you test, model people who are winners in the market right now. You can do that without copying them and without robbing from them - I didn't say that. I said *model* them, because they have money invested, too. *They* ARE watching this stuff. *They* ARE optimizing their materials.

Whether you're an ordinary guy, Joe Karbo's famous lazy man, or a woman selling to women—whoever you are, large or small, *clearly the market speaks.*

A GOOD PORTION OF MY LIFE REMAINS BEFORE ME

My mother was a woman who had seven children, a woman who married at 18 years of age and went immediately to work having kids and raising a family.

When she was in her early 50s, she went back to college to finish her nursing degree, which had been interrupted, and to make money and be independent. This was in the 1960s, and female independence was a growing movement then. She wanted and needed that. It was very admirable, of course.

But, her telling us that she was going to college and the event happening were two *radically* different things. Now, we were young, we were dumb, we'd grown up on the edge of civilization.

I'll just give you a story. When she told us, we were *all* supportive. She was what we considered an "older woman" attending the university.

This was a few years ago. Today, being in your mid-50s is not the same as being in your mid-50s in the 1960s.

Now, here's the most important thing. People would quiz her, "Why now? I mean, you're already an 'old woman'."

And she would say, "A good portion of my life has already been lived, that is true, *but* a good portion of my life remains before me."

And that was true, also.

But you know, it was more than just the college education and a job she got, it was a quality of life. The minute she picked back up where she left off, it suited her. She entered the profession she had begun in earnest those 30ish years prior... It was the *best* thing she could have ever done in that portion of her life. I cherish those photos of her and her exuberant spirit. And her years were lived with purpose, richness, and fulfillment.

Now, I will continue with the rest of the story! The first day I came home, after she entered college—I don't know, maybe I was 18—I came home and, like normal, asked, "What's for lunch, Mom?"

She says, "It's on the stove." So well, okay, I go look at the stove...and there isn't anything on the stove.

And I come back and say, "Mom, what's for lunch?" She says, "It's on the stove."

Now she's studying, she's got her books all around her. I'm obviously just a distraction. I go back to the stove; I come back again, and say, "Mom, it's *not* on the stove."

She peers over the top of her reading glasses and says, "Yes it is, it's on the back left burner," and goes back to her books. And I go back there and I see a pot, which I have never clearly connected with before. And I open the lid, and there's a bunch of hot dogs in hot water—and I knew it was going to be a horrible college experience!

Index

It has a record setting history!

"Short, regular, focused, intense, intended training sessions could mean riches and fulfillment to *you!*"

Most intelligent people agree that to get ahead, you must go the extra mile. But the amazing thing is, it takes *so little* to excel!

**After all, it's called the extra *mile*,
not the extra *100 miles!***

Apart From Massive Intention, It Didn't Take Much

Roger Bannister defied and redefined history by running the sub 4 minute mile. Exact time: 03:59.4/10's. 6 May 1954, Roger Bannister redefined human possibility by clocking in a mere 6/10's of a *second* sub 4 minutes.

And the amazing thing is that Bannister did NOT spend countless hours training... He gave it what he could in his busy pre-med schedule... A mere 30 minutes a day!!

And with that he set broke a barrier that had stood 3,000 years!

Roger Bannister
Runs sub 4 Minute Mile

Then, within 2 1/2 years of Bannister's unachievable, record-breaking sub 4 minute mile, 18 others were doing it.

It's Your Turn! And now you can run the extra mile by tuning into a sub 4 minute length daily audio or video message with incredible motivation, insights, and training in a wide variety of fields always centered around the philosophy of *The NEW Think And Grow Rich*.

The compounding of simply sub 4 minutes every day is incredible!

You, too, can defy the status quo in **short, regular, focused, intense, intended training sessions** and **redefine what's possible for you!**

It takes so little to excel. Visit the website and get started today:

www.BigBriefMoments.com

"Discover The "Secret" In A Magical Mastermind Study Of The 1937 *Original Publication* Of Napoleon Hill's Success Classic, *Think And Grow Rich*!"

Achiever's MasterMind
You actively participate in working study sessions... DESIGNED WITH THE SOLE PURPOSE OF MAKING YOU WEALTHY!

www.AchieversMasterMind.com

Includes:

1. Sixteen Achiever's MasterMind Sessions In Audio
2. Achiever's MasterMind Study Chapters
1. *Achiever's MasterMind* Study Guides

Bonuses include word-for-word transcriptions!

- How to do direct imprinting into your nervous system, so that you're driven to success!
- How to harness the awesome unseen power that has created Fortunes with one secret 6-step technique. (Takes less than 5 minutes to implement.)
- The 8-part, no-fail secret the winners in the wealth game use to... Create your own "breaks"
- And much, much more!

Digital Version – Save $$$! – Audio and print files downloadable instantly!

Physical Version - so you can feed CD's into your CD player and carry the convenient notebooks with you!

www.AchieversMasterMind.com

East-West Success MasterMind
Merging The Success Secrets Of Two Worlds

"If You're Looking For That Decided Edge That Can Accelerate You To Riches!..."

Author of *The NEW Think And Grow Rich*, Ted Ciuba, journeyed East to forge this collaboration. The entire event was captured, and is available to you now as the...

East-West Success MasterMind
www.EastWestSuccessMasterMind.com

Share the excitement that got people tuning in from Singapore, Malaysia, China, Hong Kong, Vietnam, Korea, Philippines, Thailand, India, Australia, UK, USA, Africa, and Latin America!

The purpose of the MasterMind is quite simple...

In a MasterMind study of the success philosophy outlined in the original *Think And Grow Rich*...

- To merge the BEST of both East and West to enable any willing human being, anywhere on this planet *or any other planet or moon*, to THINK WITH INTENT...
- To control and direct your thinking to receive the *natural result* of RICHES in your life!

"One of the most important days of my life was the day I began to read Think and Grow Rich." - W. Clement Stone

"I was invited to participate in the MasterMind *study of* Think And Grow Rich *by my friend Ted Ciuba. That 8-week program transformed my own Consciousness of Wealth...* - Dan Klatt

www.EastWestSuccessMasterMind.com

Who Else Would Like To Have

The NEW Think and Grow Rich
Author Ted Ciuba
Motivate and Train Your Group?

Schedule permitting, Ted Ciuba welcomes keynote, speaking and training invitations from businesses, organizations, associations, and promoters.

The quantum performance message of *The New Think And Grow Rich* and *Sub 4 Minute Extra Mile* is perfectly suited to anyone in pursuit of money, a career, sales, and a life!

Through a brief but thorough pre-event questionnaire, Ted Ciuba makes each presentation unique to each group.

To discuss opportunities and arrangements contact our organization by email at events@holomagic.com or from the website at www.ThinkRich.com

Ted Ciuba On Stage In LA

ADDITIONAL COPIES OF
THE NEW THINK AND GROW RICH
AT A DISCOUNT

This book reveals the key to unlocking your wealth, the secret formula to riches, the combination to the vault of abundance in modern terms and in modern ways.

Individuals have bought this book, looking to forge their destiny of riches. They've in turn, bought this book for their friends and family members, hoping to impart the mystical magic of its power. Suggested it to their employers, to distribute the book and train on it.

Entrepreneurs and coaches buy this book for their team members. Insurance and real estate companies buy this book for all the personnel in their organizations. Multi-level companies and all sales forces make this book required reading - to achieve outstanding success at any age. Motivators and business opportunities experts demand you read this book.

Companies have even bought this book and *given* it to their *customers*! Talk about an enlightened company!

To get a discount on multiple copies visit…

www.HoloMagic.com/ntr/multiple.html